RAISING PURPOSEFUL KIDS

Ultimate guide in setting a path of fulfillment for you kids.

Table of contents

Chapter 1

A self driven child

The concept of an autonomous, confident adolescent is inherently American. But somewhere between the self-esteem movement of the 1990s and society's seeming fixation with perfection, there's a school of thinking out there that today's youth have strayed off track.

The urge to be flawless is inevitable. Kids receive it from well-meaning parents, friends at school, and on social media. As a consequence, large numbers of young people suffer from self-doubt and worry.
The key to overcoming anxiety and becoming a confident adult is control.

Whether you have a toddler or adolescent, there are actions you can take to assist your kid take charge of his or her life and developing toward that confident, self-motivated American ideal.

Be a Consultant

What type of parent are you? If you are a "Tiger Mom" who pushes your kid to smash tennis balls six hours a day and practice piano for six hours a night, it's doubtful your youngster has much chance to be in charge of his or her life. On the other side, if you are a lenient parent, it's doubtful your kid gets an opportunity to acquire the feeling of discipline he or she needs to be autonomous and self-motivated.

There is, Stixrud believes, a parenting "sweet spot" — somewhere between authoritarian and laissez-faire, where a kid is given just the right amount of freedom and just the right amount of direction.

"Be a consultant, not a director," he urges. A "consultant" parent gives fundamental rules and structure, and as much advice as required, but does not insist on clear objectives.

Consider also your notion of "success." If you instantly see your kid as a rich banker in

New York, that's OK. But keep it to yourself. Your youngster is already confronting a society in which success is narrowly defined, Stixrud argues.

"Kids feel that if they don't have straight A's they won't get into an elite institution and that if they don't go to an elite college, they are going to have a C+ life," Stixrud adds. He laments that low-achieving students typically quit up before they start, while high-achieving youngsters lose sleep over an A-. Make sure you're helping your youngster realize the bigger options rather than further restricting the field.

Avoid Comparisons

Every kid is distinct and will demand response alterations in parenting style. Avoid comparing your youngster to his classmates — or even siblings. An older sister could flourish playing club soccer and easily receive straight A's, while her little brother would require peaceful days perched in his treehouse and get largely B's.

Stixrud points out that there is a poor association between high school grades and subsequent success.

Instead of looking around for ideals in the media, or imposing your expectations, take a hard look at your youngster. Encourage her interests. Pursuing a passion — whether for contemporary dance or rock collecting — helps a youngster to feel the gratification of working hard at something she appreciates.

Remember that your kid will change as he ages. "We have youngsters who are a catastrophe of motivation, but as their prefrontal cortex matures, they emerge out of it," Johnson adds. "A youngster could be killing it at age 10, but might not be at the top of the pack by age 30. Prodigies don't generally wind up becoming musicians. And kids who are a disaster today, are not necessarily a mess forever."

Address Anxiety

A certain level of stress may be helpful, Johnson argues. He and Stixrud term this "optimal" stress, and show that stress and rivalry enhance motivation and productivity, up to a point. “Past that point,” Johnson continues, “the fear of utterly blowing it exceeds the incentive to excel.”

If anxiety is harming you or your child’s everyday life, address it. “Stress is contagious,” Johnson explains. “It may damage the entire family.”

You can normalize tension by bringing it up at the dinner table.

“Talking about an issue you are facing is an excellent approach to offer coping mechanisms,” recommends Abby Pressel, a certified psychologist from Chapel Hill Pediatric Psychology. “You may explain practical methods you handle worry, such as concentrating on calming your muscles and managing your breathing.”

When your kid is anxious about a particular topic, listen and accept her worries. At the same time, gently question her assumptions. “Often, anxiety might be irrational,” Pressel explains. “Try to put statistics behind the fear.”

David Graham, a counselor at Davidson College, says students who effectively traverse the demands of college are those who have outlets for stress, such as a sports team, fitness class, favorite club, or religious organization. Help your youngster discover some hobby that helps him to relax.

Let Your Child Take Ownership

"Autonomy research is dramatic," Johnson adds. "There have been studies in elderly homes that demonstrate if you offer people options, they live longer."

Chapter 2

A decisive child

From a baby picking what toy to play with to a high school senior selecting a college, children of all ages must make choices. While certain judgments can appear straightforward to an adult, they might involve abilities a youngster may not have mastered. And as kids become older, the choices become more crucial and more challenging.

That's why it's crucial to help youngsters establish decision-making abilities from an early age, by providing them plenty of experience in a developmentally appropriate manner. Our experts detail how to give suitable scaffolding when they need it, and when to let them stretch their decision-making muscles on their own.

Start early – even toddlers can make judgments.

"Start teaching your young kid how to make choices by providing them two alternatives, both of which you are good with their selecting," says Grace Berman, LCSW, a clinical social worker. "For example, let them choose whether they want to wear their red shoes or blue shoes, or offer them two alternatives to choose from on a restaurant menu."

This doesn't imply that youngsters should have full freedom and make all choices – not everything needs alternatives. Continue to establish boundaries and restrictions, but offer them alternatives and freedom within those constraints. For example, kids may pick what sort of fruit they'd like for a snack, but they cannot choose to eat sugar all day.

"As they become older, explain what daily decisions you'd want your kid to be accountable for," Berman suggests. "Make a list and work with your kid to move the burden from you to them. The more judgments they can make, the more practice they will have."

Model your decision-making process

By the time we're grownups, we're so used to making choices that we may not think about the process we go through. But thinking out loud when you're making decisions — from what to prepare for dinner to where to go on vacation — might help clue youngsters into the manner you're arriving at them. What are your alternatives? What are the benefits and downsides of each?

The next stage is to include your children in a discourse about choices that impact them. For example the dilemma of whether to attend a classmate's birthday celebration or go to a different friend's home instead. Ask your youngster why they should go to the party vs the reasons not to attend. But then address how the birthday kid may feel if they knew your youngster missed the celebration to play with a buddy. The sooner you can teach youngsters to be attentive to how their actions may affect others, the better.

"It's extremely essential to engage kids in those dialogues because you're modeling a lot of really fantastic skills," says Rachel Busman, PsyD, a clinical psychologist. "You're also indicating that your child's views and opinions are important and that there are numerous elements that go into making a decision."

When modeling decision-making,
concentrate on broad questions that may help your kid understand all of the information they'll need:

What choice do I need to make?
What are my alternatives, including less-preferable ones?
What are the benefits and downsides of each choice?
Are there any regulations (school policy, curfew, etc.) I need to consider it before making my decision.
How will this choice influence others?
What is my instinct urging me to do?
How does that choice make me feel?
What's my plan B?
Provide scaffolding as they learn
When enabling children to make their own decisions, you may still offer them help to make it simpler for them.

"If the youngster is stressing over what to wear every morning, it can be anxiety-based," Berman notes. "If that's the case, then it's incredibly beneficial to not make the judgments for them. They need to practice developing that talent. Give them two alternatives and be patient so they have time to genuinely decide. Then reward them when they make the choice, particularly if they do it promptly because it promotes that behavior."

Also, help your youngster realize that certain choices are more essential than others, and sometimes it's vital to practice making rapid judgments. For example, it doesn't matter whether they select chicken fingers or spaghetti for lunch today; it's more vital they decide promptly so they're not late for their next activity. They enjoy both alternatives and they can have the other one for lunch tomorrow.

When to step back

Once you feel certain that you can trust your kid with a choice, you may move away. Small choices, such as what sort of ice cream to purchase or who to invite over for a playdate, are a terrific way to start. But don't shy away from allowing them to make some somewhat larger judgments after they've proved competent in making smaller ones. For example:

Allow children to pick out their clothing, as long as they're weather-appropriate.
Let them pick what novels they'd want to read.
Ask them to determine how they'd want to celebrate their birthday.
Sometimes it might be hard to move away, but it's crucial to communicate your trust in their improving talents. When you do this, not only are you helping your kids practice making choices, but you're also helping them mold their character by enabling them to develop the attributes that successful decision-makers possess, including:
Trust in oneself and their views
Self-confidence
Decisiveness
Thoughtfulness
Analytical thinking
Empathy
"If we offer kids modest chances to make their judgments, then they'll know what to do in those greater situations because they've received training," says Dr. Busman.

"When they come to you with a simple issue, ask them whether they truly need your aid and urge them to decide on their own. Then, you may discuss it. But for major choices, say, 'I'm so delighted you came to me. This truly feels like a medium or big choice. These are the types of things where you should come to me, so we can speak about it.'"

Older children, larger decisions.
As teens and adolescents pursue independence, they also begin to confront greater choices, which may need discussion and compromise. Dr. Busman cites the example of a teenage girl who spent hours finishing her studies and regularly clashed with her parents over housework. Instead of advising her on how to solve these difficulties, Dr. Busman worked with her to determine why she was suffering and how to make better choices.

"I asked her, 'How is your homework situation going for you? Are you happy?'" Dr. Busman explains. "She realized it wasn't working well, and we explored what stands in the way of her finishing her assignments quickly. I realized that her troubles were related to procrastination, so we devised a strategy to quit procrastinating, which included making choices about when and how to spend her time."

The confrontations with her parents were partly over her procrastination – her mom would urge her to put her clothes away, but she procrastinated. She and Dr. Busman discussed how she may bargain with her mom by considering what her mom would deem acceptable and what penalties should exist. Instead of arguing, she learned how to compromise, make meaningful judgments and keep herself responsible for an agreement.

Other significant decisions adolescents encounter, such as following their friends even when they're uncomfortable or making college selections based on other people's preferences, might benefit from a similar discourse. Help them determine whether it's working for them and then work together to establish a strategy.

Let them make stupid mistakes – and learn from them

You shouldn't always rush in if you observe your kid making a wrong choice Because youngsters typically learn best from their errors. As long as it's a safe environment, let them make poor judgment. But, also consider when kids may learn more by you chiming in. It's a thin line between letting kids develop, and rescuing them when required.

For example, don't rescue your kid if they:

Would want to wear goofy attire to school. As long as it's weather-appropriate, let them. If they are mocked, they may opt not to do it again.

Choose to play a video game before soccer practice and don't have enough time to get ready. If they come to the field without their jersey, don't bring it to them.

Want to spend their allowance money on an item that breaks easily or will fast become dull?

Prefer to spend their time chatting to friends instead of preparing for an exam.

Once they've faced the penalty, help them learn from it. Remain cool, avoid assigning blame, and let them assess and learn from errors. Even if they regret the choice they made, strive to develop their decision making confidence.

"Validate their feelings and that it didn't truly turn out the way they expected," Dr. Busman recommends. "Parents frequently wish to shelter their kids from terrible emotions, yet those painful sensations provide us feedback to help us make the correct choices. They're not hazardous. We need to let them feel the repercussions of wrong actions and work through them. That's how we're going to assist our kids to become adults in the world."

Chapter 3

A self confident child

Right from infancy, babies develop new skills at a dizzying pace. And along with those new talents, they also develop the courage to employ them.

As youngsters become older, that confidence might be as crucial as the talents themselves. To flourish, youngsters need to believe in their skills but, at the same time, understand that they can manage it if they aren't successful at anything. It's through experiencing mastery and recovering from failure that kids acquire healthy self-confidence.

Here are ways you may set youngsters up to feel competent and get the most mileage out of their abilities and talents.

. Model confidence yourself

Even if you're not exactly feeling it! Seeing you handle new projects with positivity and plenty of preparation provides a positive example for youngsters. That doesn't mean you have to pretend to be flawless. Do recognize your nervousness, but don't dwell on it—focus on the good things you are doing to be ready.

. Don't get irritated about errors

Help youngsters recognize that everyone makes mistakes and the essential thing is to learn from them, not linger on them. Confident individuals don't allow fear of failure to get in their way—not because they're convinced they won't ever fail, but because they know how to accept setbacks in stride.

. Encourage them to try new things

Instead of spending all their concentration on what they currently excel at, youngsters need to diversify. Attaining new abilities lets youngsters feel competent and assured that they can conquer anything that comes their way.

. Allow kids to fail

It's natural to want to shelter your child from failure, but trial and error are how kids learn, and falling short of a goal helps kids figure out that it's not deadly. It may also drive youngsters to greater effort, which will serve them well as adults.

. Praise persistence

Learning not to quit up at the first irritation or bail after one setback is a vital life skill. Confidence and self-esteem are not about winning at everything all the time, they're about being tough enough to keep trying, and not being disturbed if you're not the greatest.

. Help students discover their passion

Exploring their hobbies may help
youngsters establish a sense of identity, which is vital to growing confidence. Of course, witnessing their abilities flourish will also offer a significant boost to their self-esteem.

. Set objectives

Articulating objectives, big and little, and accomplishing them helps youngsters feel powerful. Help your kid transform wishes and ambitions into achievable goals by encouraging them to write a list of things they'd like to achieve. Then, try breaking down longer-term objectives into attainable milestones. You'll be recognizing their interests and helping them gain the skills they'll need to reach their objectives throughout life.

. Celebrate effort

Praising kids for their successes is excellent, but it's equally crucial to let them know you're happy with their efforts regardless of the result. It takes hard effort to build new talents, and results aren't always quick. Let kids know you admire the effort they're doing, whether they're infants constructing with blocks or adolescents training themselves to play the guitar.

. Expect them to throw in

They can moan, but youngsters feel more connected and valued when they're called on to complete age-appropriate activities, from tidying up toys to washing dishes to collecting up younger siblings after a play date. Homework and after-school activities are excellent, but are needed by your family.

. Embrace imperfection

As grown-ups, we know perfection is unachievable, and kids must hear that message as early as possible. Help youngsters recognize that whether it's on TV, in a magazine, or on a friend's social media account, the concept that others are always happy, successful, and flawlessly dressed is a dream and a damaging one. Instead, tell them that being less than flawless is human and perfectly alright.

. Set them up for success

Challenges are excellent for youngsters, but they should also have chances where they can be guaranteed to achieve success. Help your youngster become engaged with things that help him feel comfortable and confident enough to handle a greater task.

. Show your affection

Let your kid know you adore him no matter what. Win or lose the big game, excellent grades or terrible. Even when you're upset with him. Making sure your kid understands that you think they're terrific — and not only when they achieve fantastic things — can reinforce their self-worth even when they're not feeling good about themselves.

Chapter 4

A responsible child

We all want to raise responsible children. And we all want to live in a society where others have been taught to be responsible, a world where grownups don’t shrug off their obligations as citizens. As my kid asked, observing the trashed park when he was four, "Don't adults realize they have to pick up their messes?"

So how do we train our kids to accept responsibility for their choices and their influence on the world?

You begin by viewing responsibility as something delightful for your kid, instead of a burden. All youngsters want to perceive themselves as response-able — strong and able to react to what has to be done. They need this for their self-worth, and for their life to have significance. Children don't want only to be doted on. They need, like the rest of us, to feel like they matter to the world, and that their lives make a meaningful contribution.

You don't need to educate kids to manage themselves appropriately in the world; you only need to show them that they have the potential to contribute positively and to connect to them so that they desire to do so.

The basic truth is that kids will be responsible to the degree that we assist them to be. Here are 12 common tactics sure to boost your kids' "response-ability" quotient.

1. Raise your youngster with the assumption that we always clean up our messes.

Begin by assisting your kid, till she learns it. She'll learn it quickly if you can be pleasant and nice about it and remember not to fret over spilled milk. Encourage her to assist by giving her a sponge as you pick one up yourself, even though it's quicker to do it yourself. (And it's nearly always simpler to do it yourself.) As long as you aren't judgemental about it—so she isn't defensive—she'll want to help clean up and make things better.

So when your kid spills her milk, remark "Oops, milk spilled. That's fine. We can clean it up," as you offer her a paper towel and pick one up yourself. When your preschooler leaves her shoes strewn in your path, offer them to her and urge her to put them away, stating nicely "We always tidy up our things."

You will have to do this, in one form or another, until they leave your house. But if your attitude is cheerful and light-hearted, your youngster won't become defensive and complain that you should do the cleaning. And when youngsters hear the continual cheerful expectation that "We always clean up our messes...Don't worry, I'll assist.... Here are the paper towels for you; I'll fetch the sponge..." people become both easier to live with and better citizens of the world.

2. Kids need a chance to contribute to the common good.

All youngsters give to the rest of us in some manner, consistently. Find those ways and remark on them, even if it is only observing when she is sweet to her younger brother or that you appreciate how she’s constantly singing. Whatever habits you recognize will develop.

As your children become older, their contributions may rise properly, both inside and beyond the home. Kids need to develop two sorts of responsibilities: their self-care, and contributing to the family welfare. Research reveals that youngsters who assist around the home are also more inclined to provide aid in other circumstances than kids who merely engage in their self-care.

Of all, you can't expect them to have a helping attitude overnight. It helps to slowly build responsibility in age-appropriate ways. Invite toddlers to arrange napkins on the table, and three-year-olds to set seats. Four-year-olds can match socks, and five-year-olds can assist you to groom the dog. Six-year-olds are ready to clear the table, seven-year-olds to water plants, and eight-year-olds to fold clothes. Again, note that you're welcoming and empowering your kid, not guilting and burdening them.

3. Remember that no youngster in his right mind wants to perform "chores."

Unless you want your kid to think of contributing to the family as drudgery, don't "make" him perform tasks without you until they are a normal part of your family routine and one that your youngster does not resent. Your goal isn't getting this specific job done, it's shaping a child who will take pleasure in contributing and taking responsibility. Make the work entertaining. Give as much structure, support, and hands-on aid as you need to, even sitting with him and assisting for the first thirty times he performs the job if required. Know that it will be considerably tougher than doing it yourself. Remind yourself that there's a delight in these jobs, and transmit that, along with the satisfaction of a job well done. Eventually, he will be completing these duties by himself. That day will come much sooner if he likes them.

4. Always let them "do it myself" and "help" even though it's more work for you.

And it will always be more effort for you. But toddlers desire urgently to manage their physical environments, and when we help them to achieve so, they step into the responsibility of being "response-able." So instead of speeding through your list, reframe. You're working with your youngster to help him find the joy of participation. That's more essential than getting the work done swiftly or properly. Notice that you're also connecting, which is what inspires youngsters to keep giving.

5.Rather than merely issuing command, invite your youngsters To think

For instance, to the dallying toddler in the morning, instead of yelling "Brush your teeth! Is your backpack packed? Don't forget your lunch!," you may ask "What's the next thing you need to do to be ready for school?" The idea is to keep them focused on their list, morning after morning until they absorb it and begin handling their daily duties.

6. Provide routines and structure.
These are vital in children's lives for many reasons, not the least of which is that it allows them repeated opportunity to manage themselves through a succession of not very attractive chores. First, they master the nighttime routine including tidying up toys and getting dressed in the morning. Then kids build excellent study habits and grooming routines. Finally, students acquire fundamental living skills via the repetition of daily chores like washing laundry or creating simple meals.

7.Teach your kid to be accountable for her relationships with others by utilizing repair instead of punishment.
When your daughter harms her younger brother's emotions, don't compel her to apologize. She won't mean it, and it won't help him. First, listen to her feelings to help her work out those tangled emotions that made her snarl at him. Then, after she feels better, ask her what she can do to make

things right between them. Maybe she'll be ready to apologize. But maybe that will feel like losing face, and she would rather repair things with him by reading him a story or helping him with his chore of setting the table or giving him a big hug. This teaches children that their treatment of others has a cost and that they're always responsible for repairs when they do damage. But because you aren't forcing her, she's able to CHOOSE to make the repair, which makes it feel good, and makes her more likely to repeat it.

What if your kid refuses repair? That stems from anger, or what we may term "a chip on the shoulder." Your kid feels like the one who has been injured or offended and hence won't start the mending process because she believes that her actions were merited — if not by what occurred in this event, then surely by earlier complaints. That's a greater healing effort that you'll need to be part of, so start now by creating trust, listening to your child's upsets, and addressing those old sentiments. This teaches your kid that you care, they aren't alone, and they may experience those old feelings and get through them. But at the same time as you're encouraging your kid to heal their previous misery, urge that they fix present relations.

8. Support your youngster to help pay for damaged stuff.

If youngsters help pay from their allowance for missing library books and mobile phones, windows damaged by their baseball, or tools they've left out to rust, the odds of a repeat offense are limited.

9. Don't hurry to bail your youngster out of a terrible situation.

Be accessible for issue-solving, helping him work through his thoughts and worries, and to assure that he doesn't merely skirt the difficulties, but allows him to face the situation himself, whether it needs expressing an apology or making apologies more tangibly.

10. Model responsibility and accountability

Be specific about the responsible decisions you're making:

"It's a bother to carry this rubbish until we get to the vehicle, but I don't see a trashcan and we never litter."

"This sign states parking is intended for those with physical problems, so of course, we can't use that place."

Keep your commitments to your kid, and don't create excuses. If you don't follow through when you promise to pick up that notebook he needs for school or play that game with him on Saturday, why should he be responsible for maintaining his commitments and agreements with you?

11. Never label your child as "irresponsible"

Never classify your child as "Irresponsible," since the way we perceive our kids is always a self-fulfilling prophecy. Instead, teach him the skills he needs to be responsible. If he constantly loses stuff, for instance, educate him to stop every time he goes someplace — his friend's house, school, soccer practice —

and check off everything he needs to carry home.

12. Teach your youngster to develop a documented schedule.

It may sound like overkill, but in our busy 21st-century life, all pupils need to master this ability by high school, or they just won't get anything done. Begin on weekends throughout middle school, or sooner, if their schedule is hectic. Just grab a piece of paper, put the hours of the day on the left, and ask your kid what he needs to get done this weekend. Put in the baseball game, piano practice, the birthday celebration, and all the processes of the scientific project - shop for supplies to create the volcano, and write and print out the description. Be careful to block off downtime — go for ice cream with dad, unwind and listen to music. Most youngsters think this keeps their stress level down, as they know when everything will get done. Most importantly, it teaches students to manage their time and be responsible for their responsibilities.

Chapter 5

A child with a healthy sense of Identity

Identity, in general, is the process of recognizing oneself and discovering that we have an essential position in the world around us. It may seem very weird, but infants establish a sense of identity from a fairly early age. The feeling of identity begins forming from a young age and with the active involvement of those that are continually in contact with the youngsters. They do think about replies relating to who they are and how the others around them see them. They keep asking questions to get their answers. They are conscious of being able to accomplish anything and so, enjoy modest victories.

How do Children Develop Identity?

It all starts when youngsters discover that we are all born as different people. Once that sense of self becomes formed, youngsters learn that they too have a place in this world, even if they are different from others. We are varied in our body, gender, size, and talents and consequently, they learn that we all have a place in this world.

But not all youngsters could be excellent at finding their sense of identity. That's where the parents and the school come in. Here is a list of measures that might assist you to establish a sense of identity in your children.

Be present for the child-

Pay great attention to your youngster. Answer their inquiries and encourage them to gain a deeper image of themselves. Help them to communicate when they appear to be stuck. Acknowledge their modest successes and let them know that they are cherished.

Encourage your kid-

Encourage your youngster to make choices and decisions. Encourage them to solve difficulties and to keep going once things start becoming tough. Let them attempt things that they look forward to. Help them in their pursuit of becoming independent. This will assist to create self-confidence in them.

Instill values in your child-

Focus on fundamental principles like honesty, hard effort, respect, compassion, morality, and responsibility. Make them acquainted with the relevance of these ideals. Teach children to be polite and sensitive to seniors and even to youngsters who are younger than them. There are kids' education applications and games accessible online, you can always utilize them.

Introduce them to self-care and self-love-

One of the most crucial aspects in building a sense of identity is being acquainted with oneself and to esteem oneself. Remind them that they are lovely and essential in their way. Help them in emphasizing their natural abilities and developing them for success.

www.ingramcontent.com/pod-product-compliance
Lightning Source LLC
LaVergne TN
LVHW050009180826
845678LV00022B/3469

* 9 7 9 8 8 4 8 2 0 7 4 1 5 *